Tanks, Aircraft & Armored Vehicles

Learn to draw 23 favorite subjects, Step by easy step, shape by simple shape!

Illustrated by Tom LaPadula

Associate Publisher: Elizabeth T. Gilbert
Art Director: Shelley Baugh
Managing Editor: Rebecca J. Razo
Associate Editor: Emily Green
Production Artist: Debbie Aiken, Rae Siebels

www.walterfoster.com
Walter Foster Publishing, Inc.
3 Wrigley, Suite A
Irvine, CA 92618

1 3 5 7 9 10 8 6 4 2

Table of Contents

Getting Started

When you look closely at the drawings in this book, you'll notice that they're made up of basic shapes, such as circles, ovals, and triangles. To draw all your favorite military machines, just start with simple shapes as you see here. It's easy and fun!

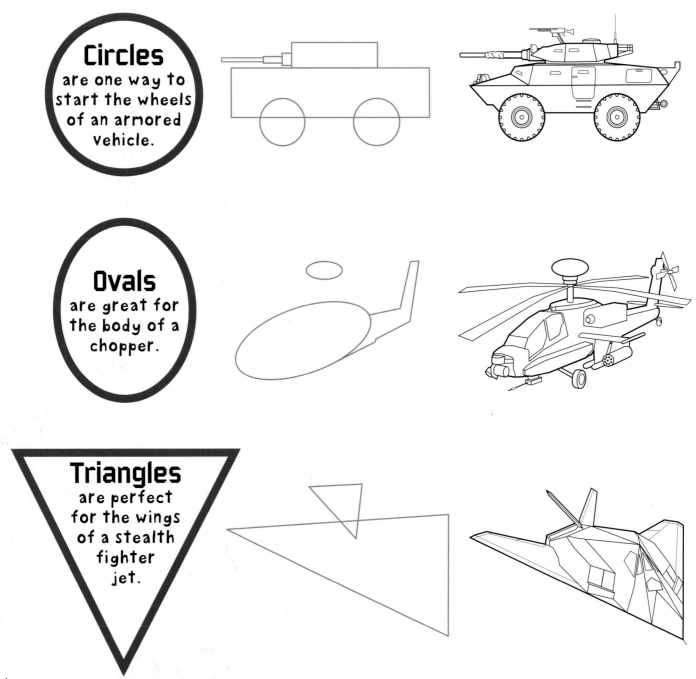

Circles are one way to start the wheels of an armored vehicle.

Ovals are great for the body of a chopper.

Triangles are perfect for the wings of a stealth fighter jet.

Tools & Materials

Before you begin, gather some drawing tools, such as paper, a regular pencil, an eraser, and a pencil sharpener. For color, you can use markers, colored pencils, paint, crayons, or even colored chalk.

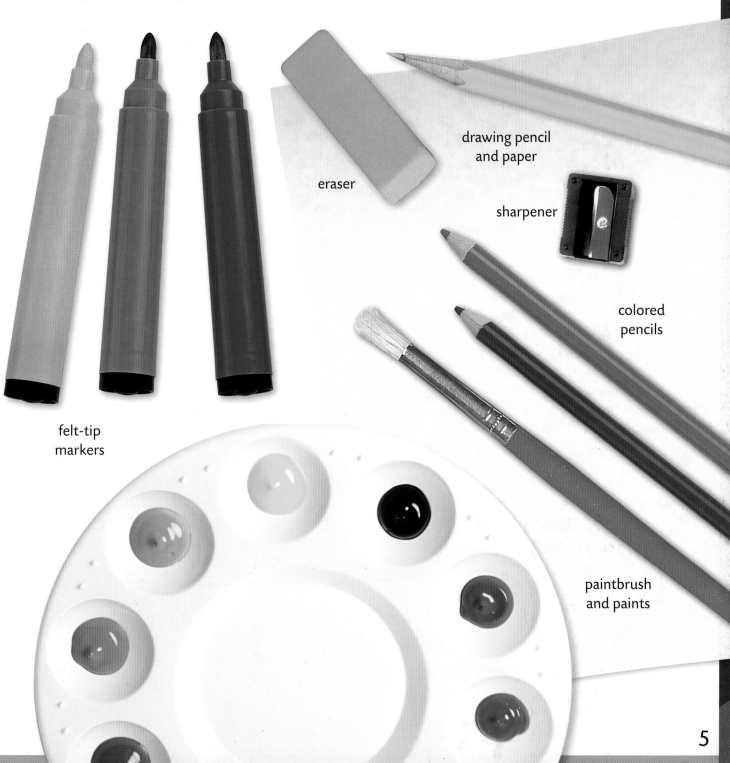

drawing pencil and paper

eraser

sharpener

colored pencils

felt-tip markers

paintbrush and paints

Twin-Engine Attack Helicopter

A power-packed chopper with a chain gun and rockets,
this aircraft is designed for close-combat missions.

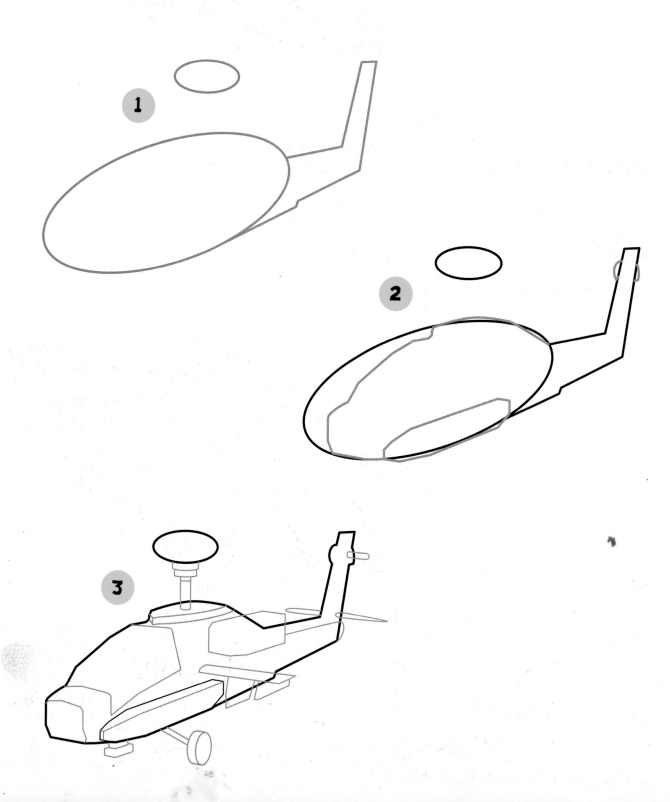

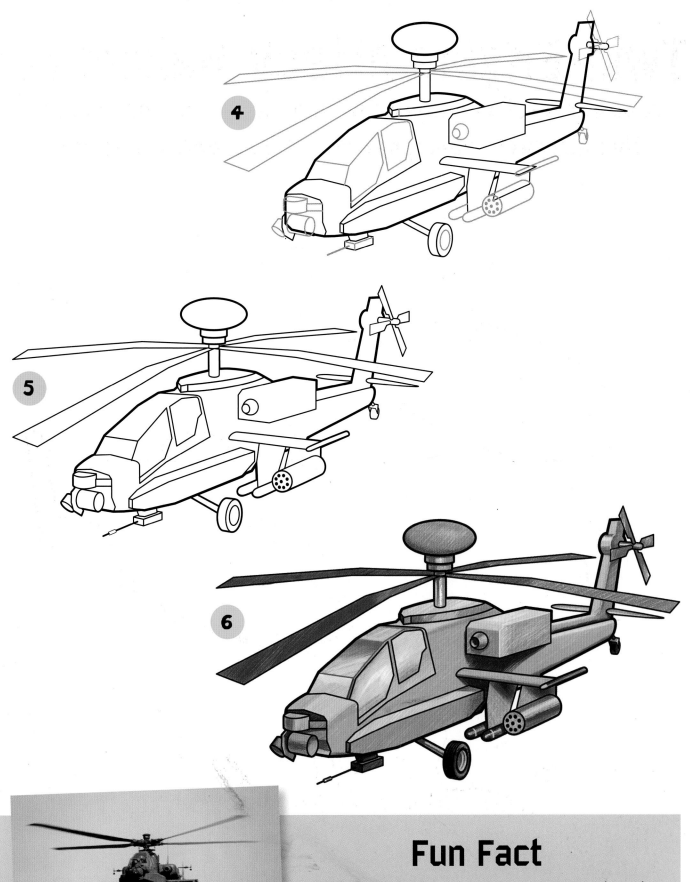

4

5

6

Fun Fact

This chopper's two-person crew can navigate and attack targets using night vision. It can even continue flying after hits from powerful artillery shells.

Military Transport Aircraft

This plane carries troops and equipment thousands of miles across the ocean. It can haul up to 500,000 pounds!

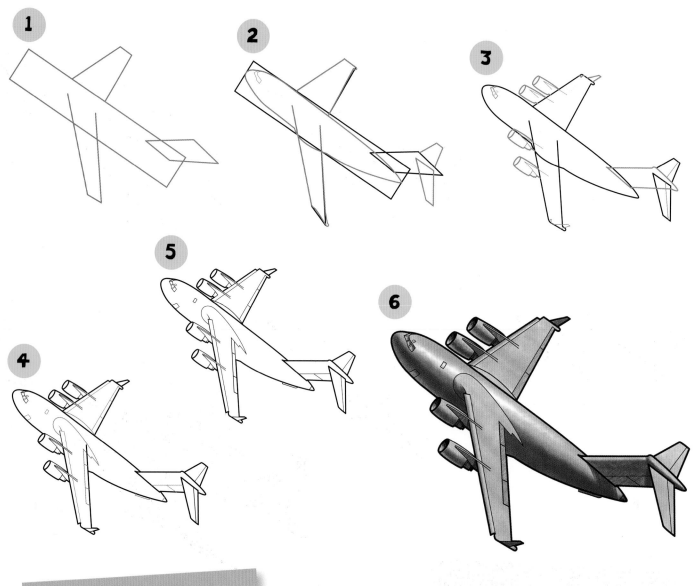

1

2

3

5

4

6

Fun Fact

Despite its large size, this aircraft is designed to land on short runways quickly and efficiently. A three-person crew helps load cargo and troops through a rear ramp. Tanks and trucks simply drive right into it!

Airborne Warning and Control System (AWACS)

An **AWACS** is a radar dish covered in a special damage-resistant case that attaches to the top of an aircraft.

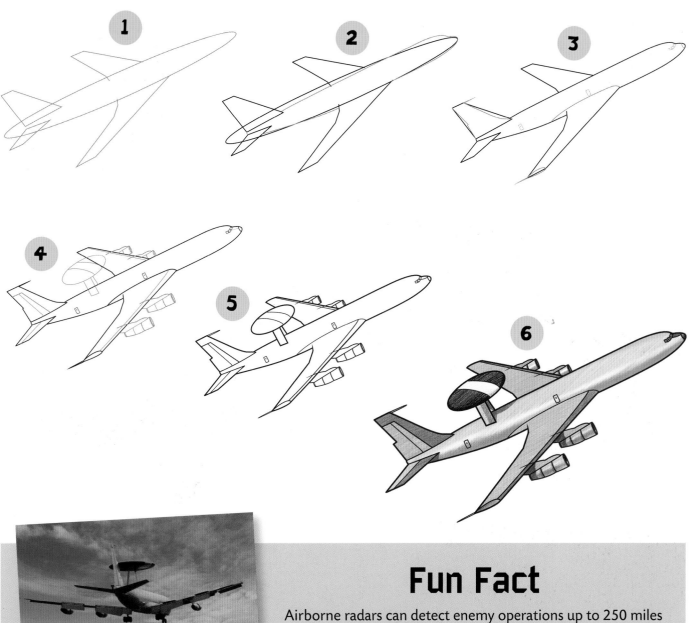

Fun Fact

Airborne radars can detect enemy operations up to 250 miles away, as well as high up in the stratosphere. They can track airplanes, ships, and cruise missiles. They are used by many different countries and can also be attached to helicopters.

High Mobility Multipurpose Wheeled Vehicle (HUMVEE)

Before it became a consumer sport-utility vehicle, this diesel-fueled machine was used for military purposes.

Fun Fact

These tough trucks are used as ambulances, troop and cargo carriers, and missile launchers. Combat helicopters can deliver them wherever they need to go.

Vertical/Short Takeoff and Landing Aircraft

This may look like a normal jet, but it's full of surprises—
it can take off and land just like a helicopter.

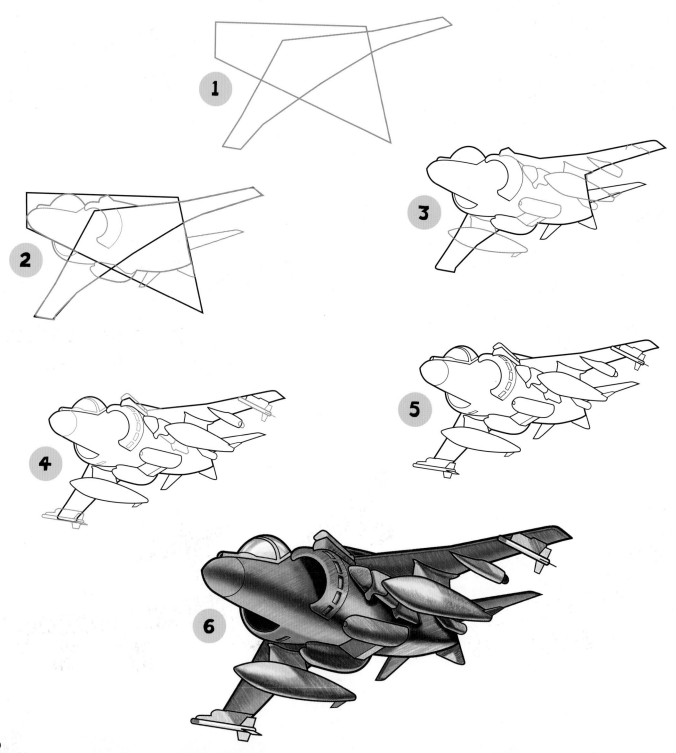

B-52 Bomber

Powered by eight turbo-jet engines, this behemoth bomber can carry up to 70,000 pounds of weapons.

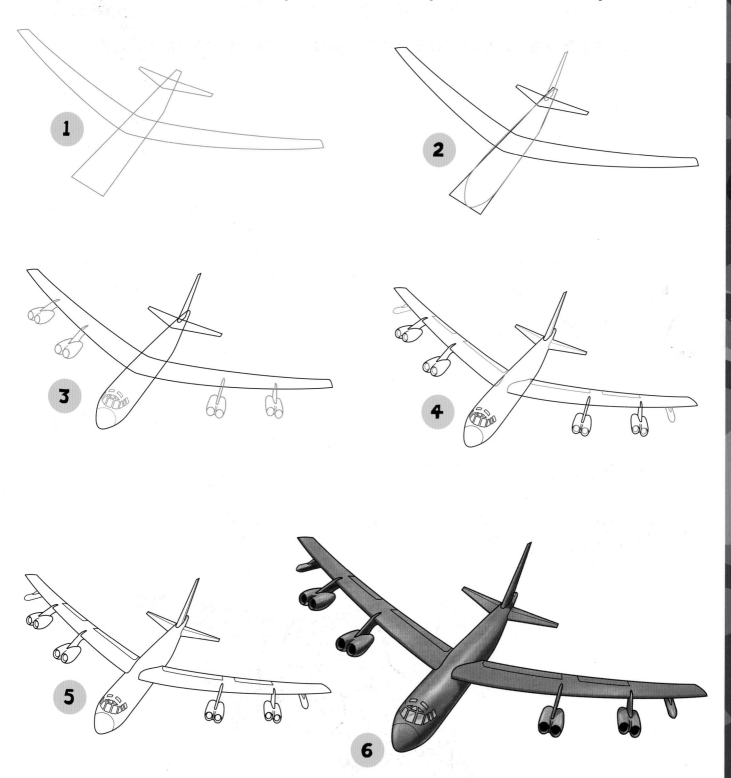

Black Hawk
Twin-Engine Helicopter

with its three-person crew, the Black Hawk can transport a fully equipped 11-man infantry squad.

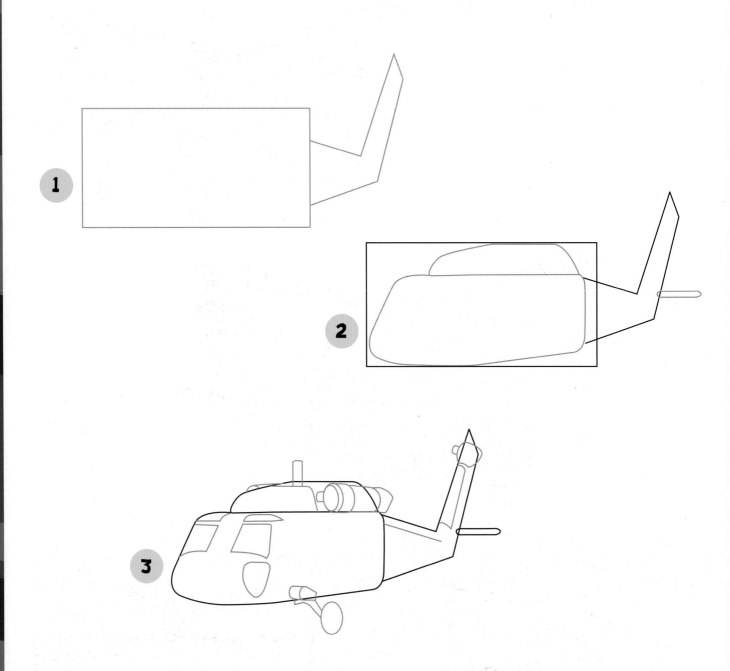

4

5

6

Fun Fact

A multifaceted war machine, Black Hawks have two machine guns fitted to their doors and can withstand hits from heavy artillery.

M1 Abrams Battle Tank

A 1,500-horsepower engine, three machine guns, and a 120mm smoothbore cannon make this tank one tough trooper!

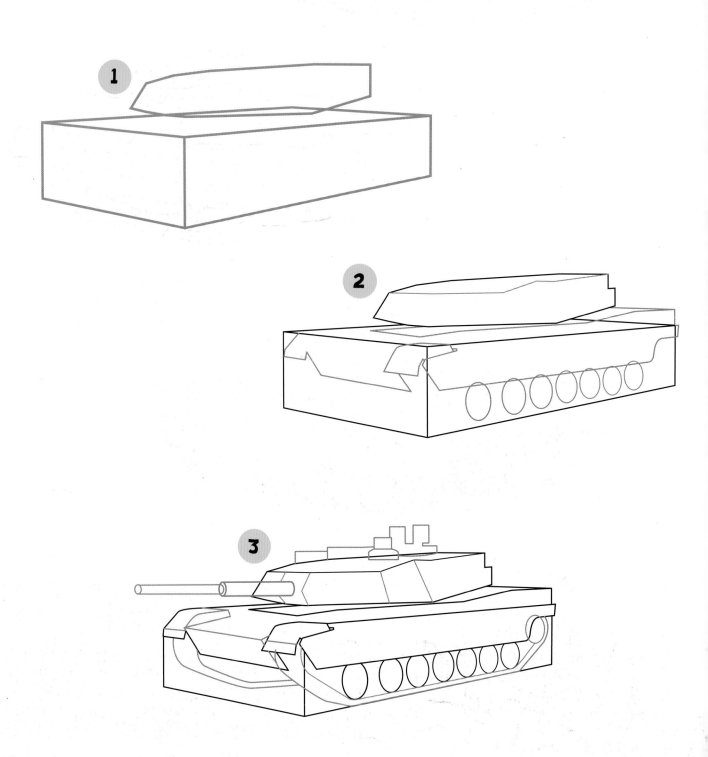

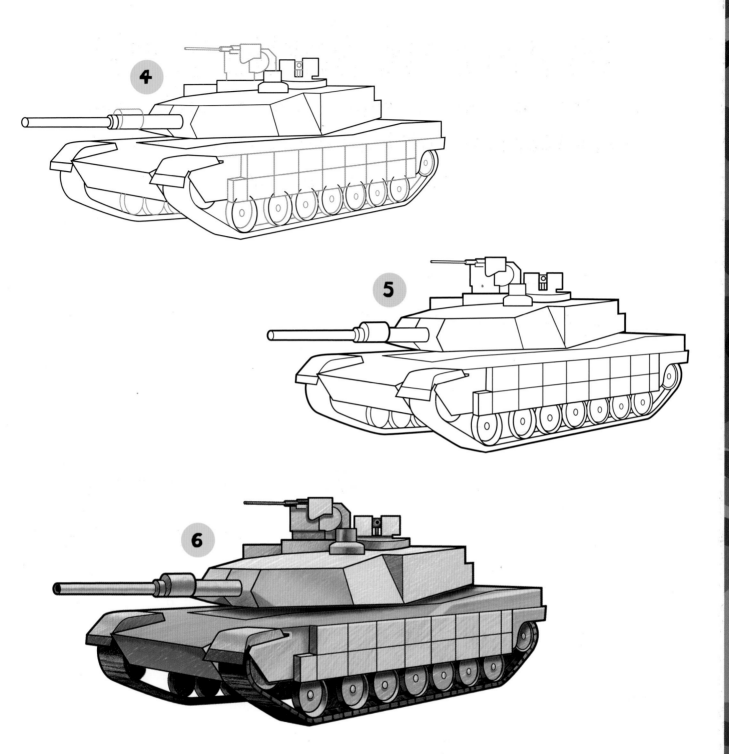

4

5

6

Fun Fact

The M1 is fitted with special ceramic and metal armor that protects it from anti-tank weapons. In fact, this battle tank is strong enough to survive a nuclear explosion!

Stealth Fighter Jet

This sneak-attack jet may look bizarre, but its triangular shape helps it escape radar detection.

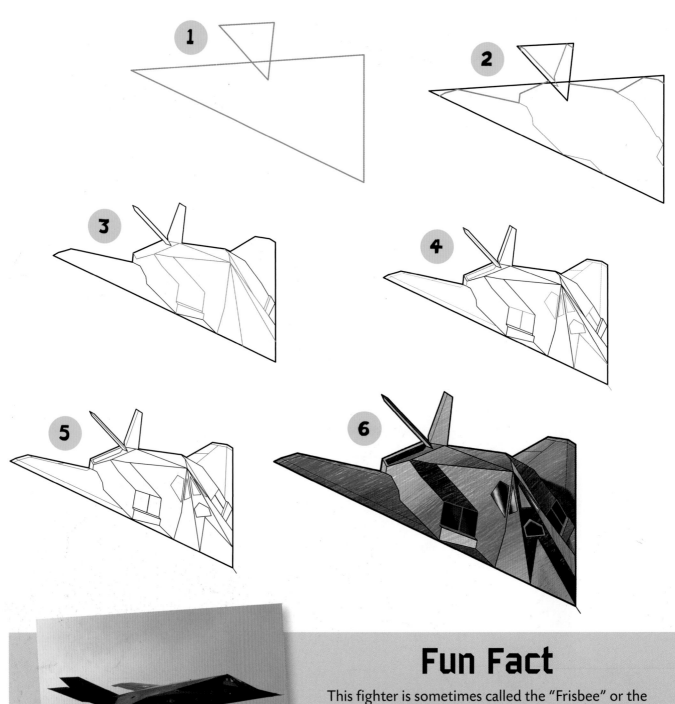

Fun Fact

This fighter is sometimes called the "Frisbee" or the "Wobblin' Goblin." Despite its ability to fly "under the radar," the aircraft was retired in 2008.

Stealth Ship

Just like the stealth fighter jet, the stealth ship can hide from radar detection thanks to its unique shape.

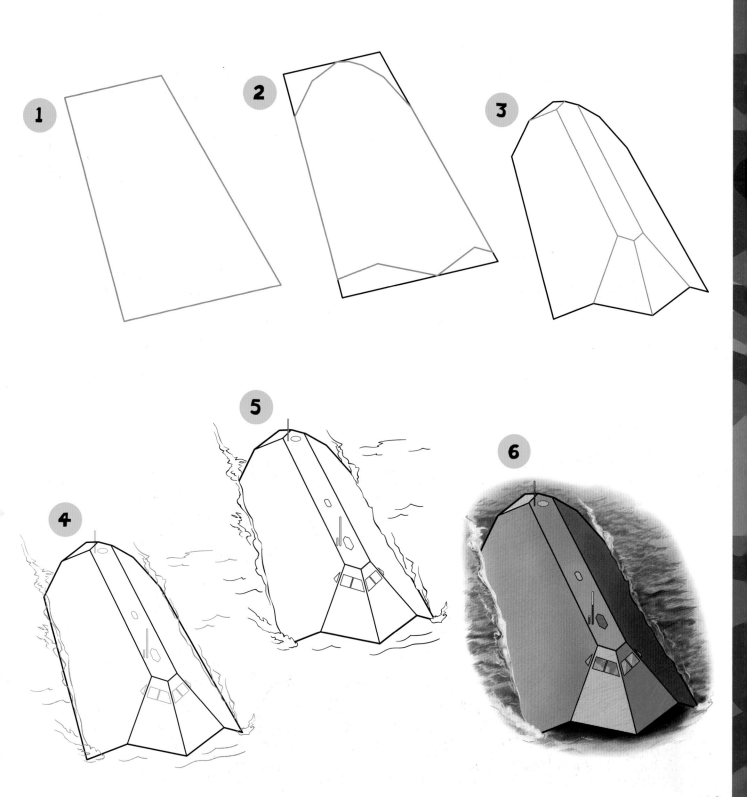

Amphibious Armored Car

This multi-use car is "amphibious" because it travels across both rivers and battlefields with ease. It's used as an ambulance, anti-tank vehicle, and troop carrier.

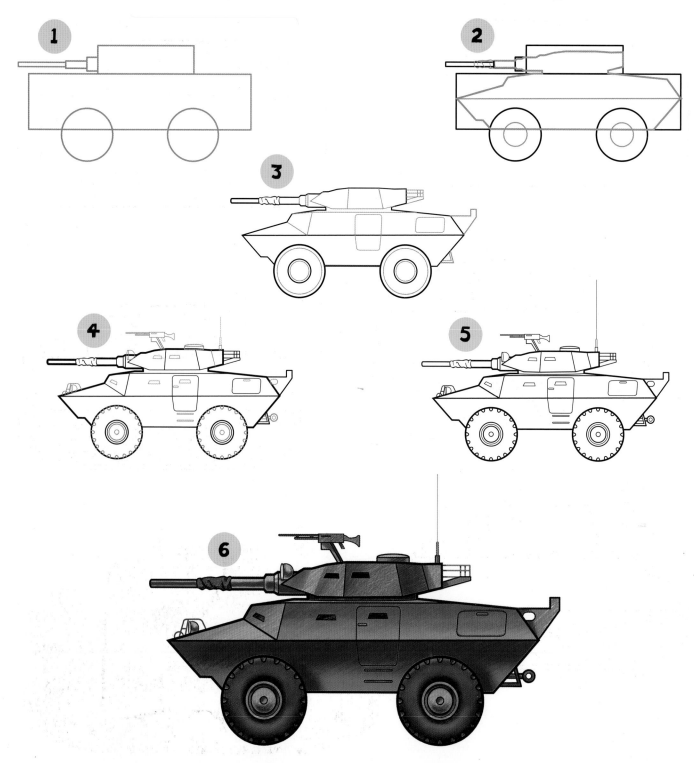

M113 Family of Vehicles

The M113 is the most popular armored vehicle in the world. About 80,000 are used in more than 50 countries!

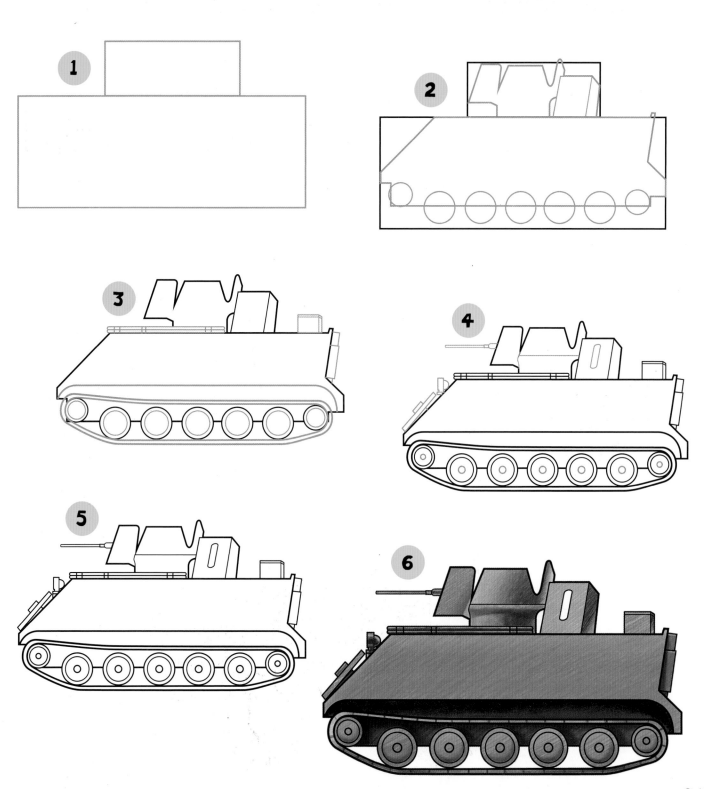

F-14

This fighter jet can carry up to 13,000 pounds of missiles. At the touch of a button, the pilot can change the angle of its wings to make it fly faster or slower.

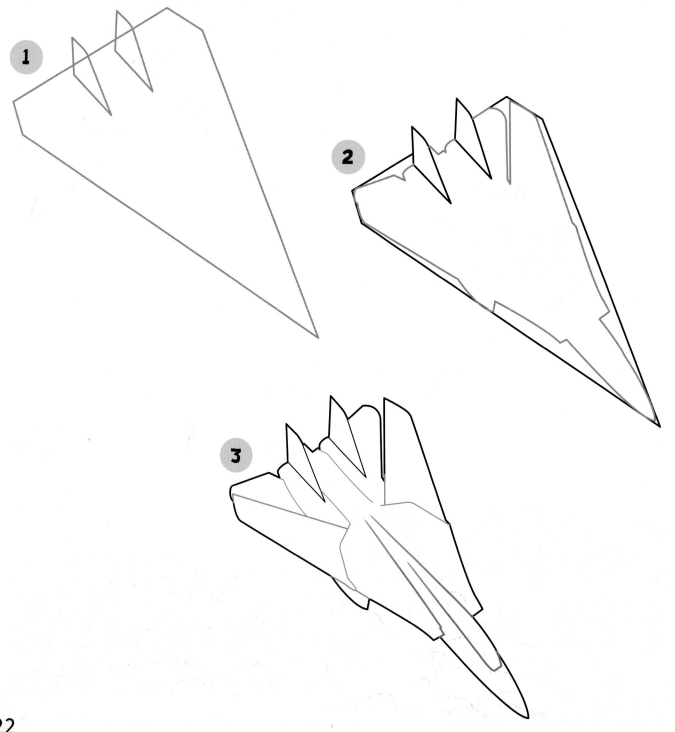

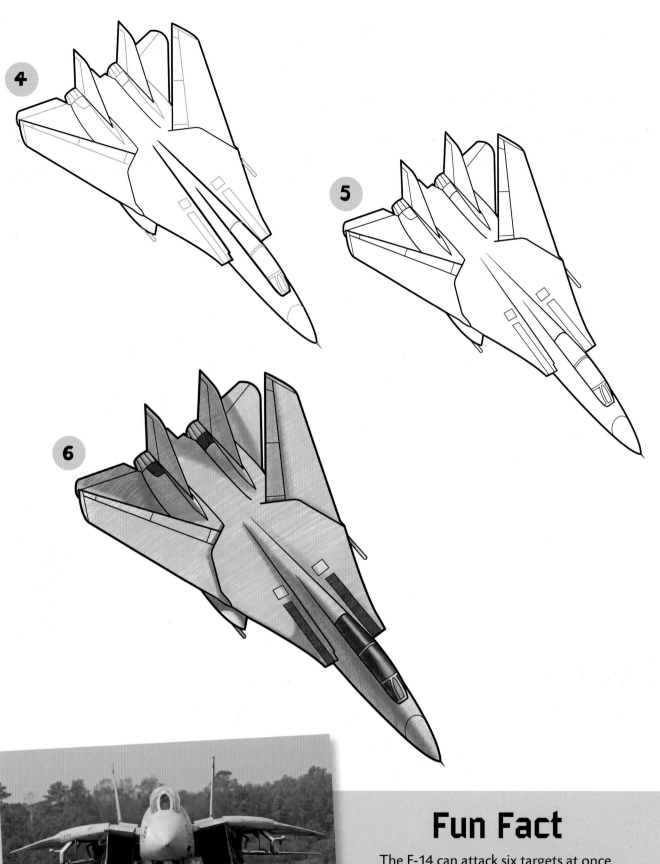

4

5

6

Fun Fact

The F-14 can attack six targets at once.
It's even capable of shooting down
another fighter plane or a cruise missile.

Tandem-Rotor Heavy-Lift Helicopter

This combat helicopter can transport **44** soldiers and travel more than **330** miles in a single trip.

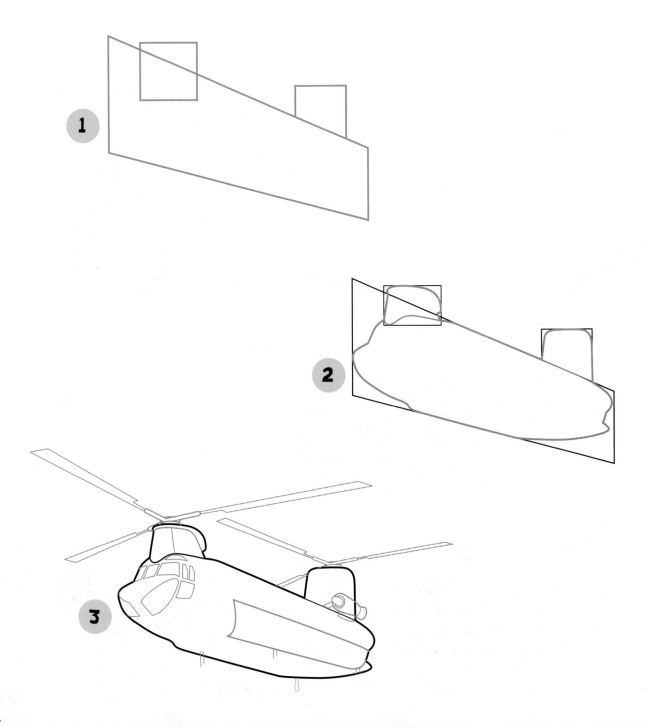

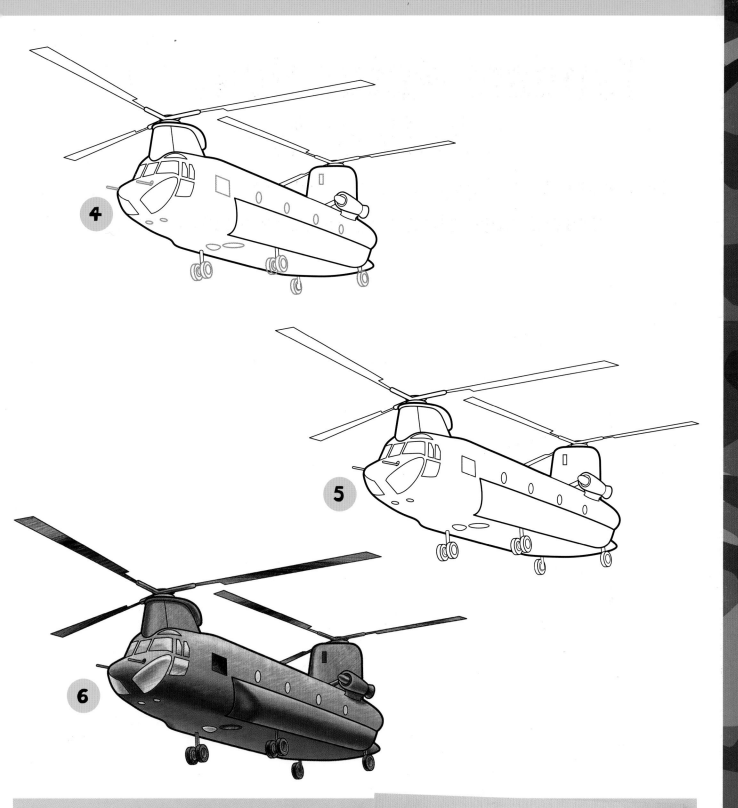

Fun Fact

This muscular helicopter is strong enough to carry two 5,000-pound HUMVEEs—the vehicles drive right onto the craft through its rear ramp. Three cargo hooks attached to its underside allow it to haul up to 26,000 pounds!

Armored Combat Vehicle

This mean green fighting machine is packed with heavy-duty weapons and wrapped in a rough and tough armor.

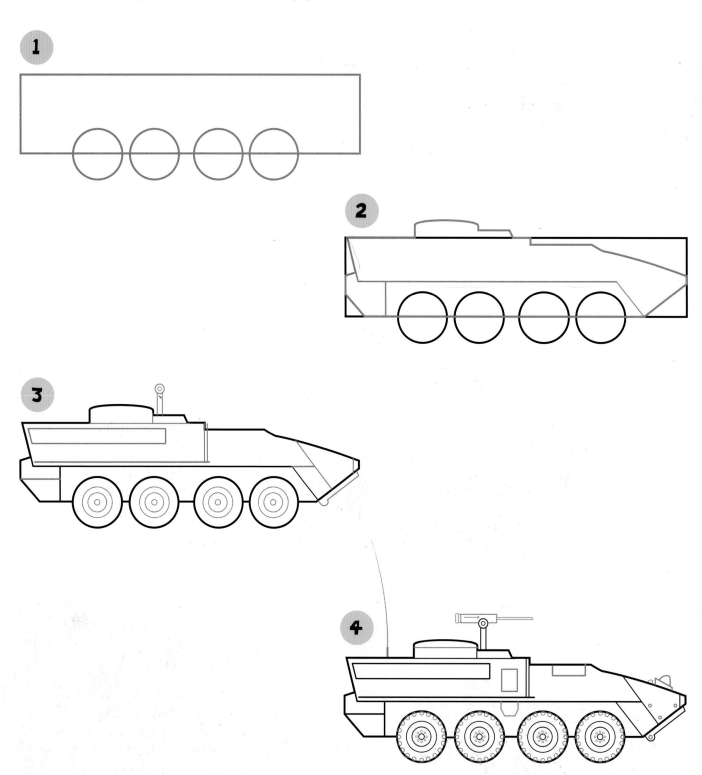

5

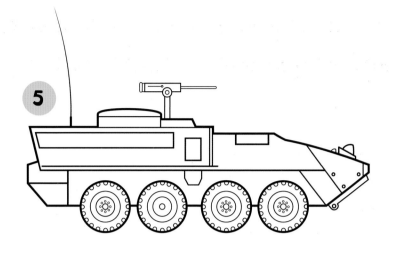

6

Fun Fact

This vehicle protects troops from improvised explosive devices (IEDs)—tiny bombs placed underground. IEDs tend to destroy most vehicles, but not this one—it can withstand almost anything!

Guided Missile Submarine

This ferocious vessel runs on nuclear power. It can carry **154** land-attack cruise missiles or **24** nuclear warheads.

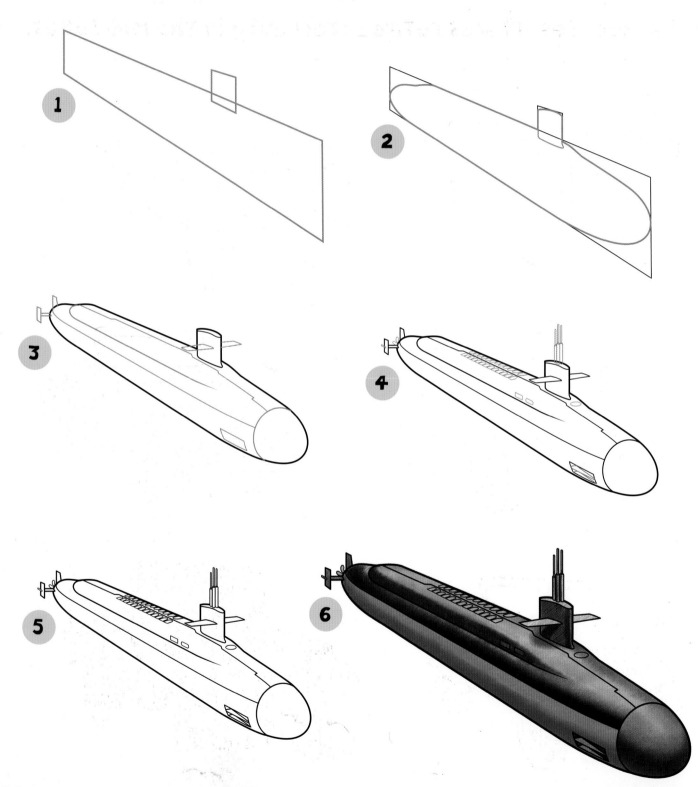

Four-Wheel-Drive Utility Vehicle

This open-air vehicle was the U.S. military's go-to truck for decades. It was retired from duty in the mid-1980s.

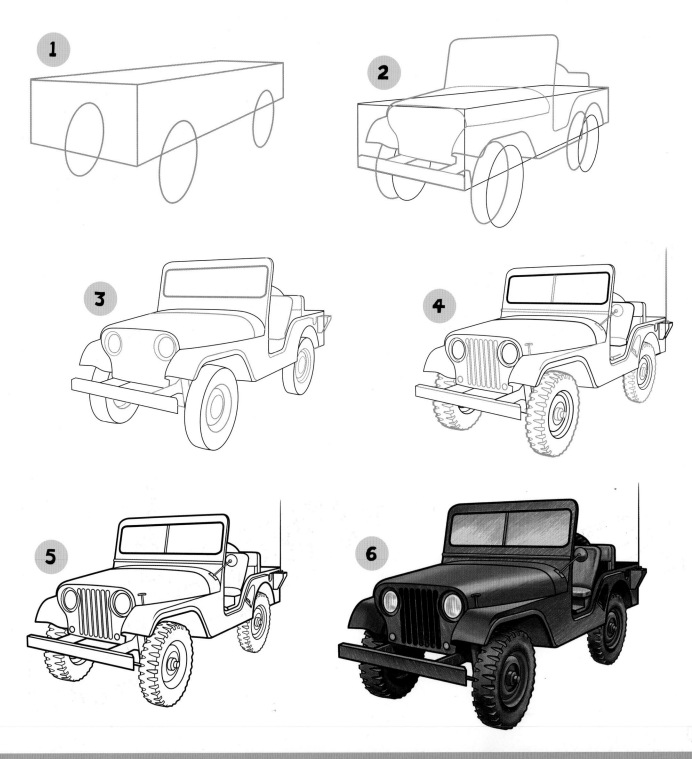

M36 Tank Destroyer

Used in during WWII, the M36 featured an anti-tank gun that could destroy other tanks up to 10 miles away.

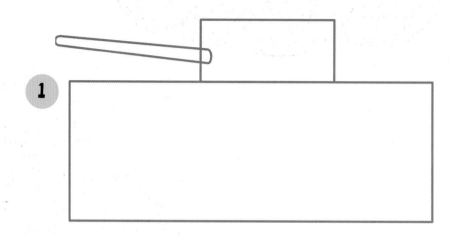

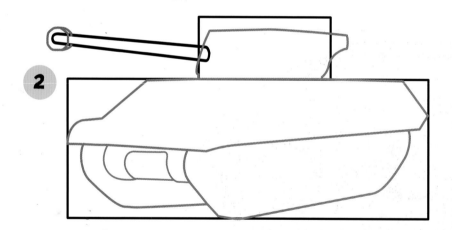

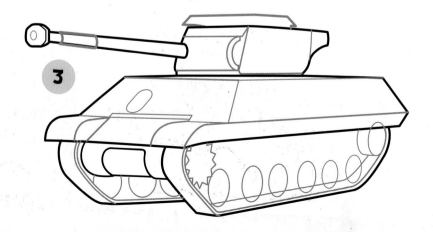

4

5

6

Fun Fact

The original tank destroyers had an open turret: a rotating platform on top of the tank that protected the gunner and crew. Modern tanks feature covered turrets.

Tilt-Rotor Vertical/Short Takeoff and Landing Aircraft

The bulky gray aircraft is a real-life transformer: It can turn itself into an airplane AND a helicopter.

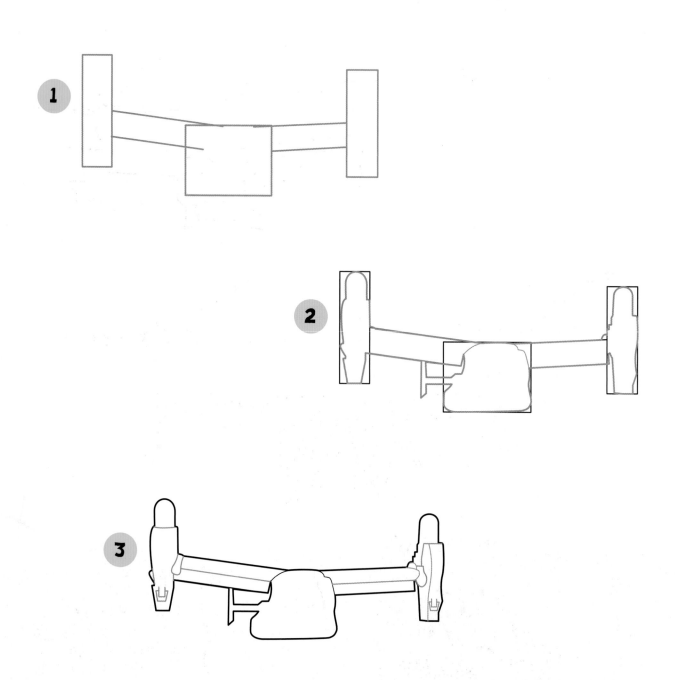

4

5

6

Fun Fact

This helicopter can do things planes only dream about. Like a helicopter, it can carry up to 15,000 pounds of cargo on two external hooks, and it can take off and land without a runway. Like a plane, it's able to cruise 30,000 feet above sea level for more than 2,000 miles—without refueling!

F-16

This single-engine, single-pilot fighter jet is small, light, and quick. It flies at supersonic neck-breaking speeds!

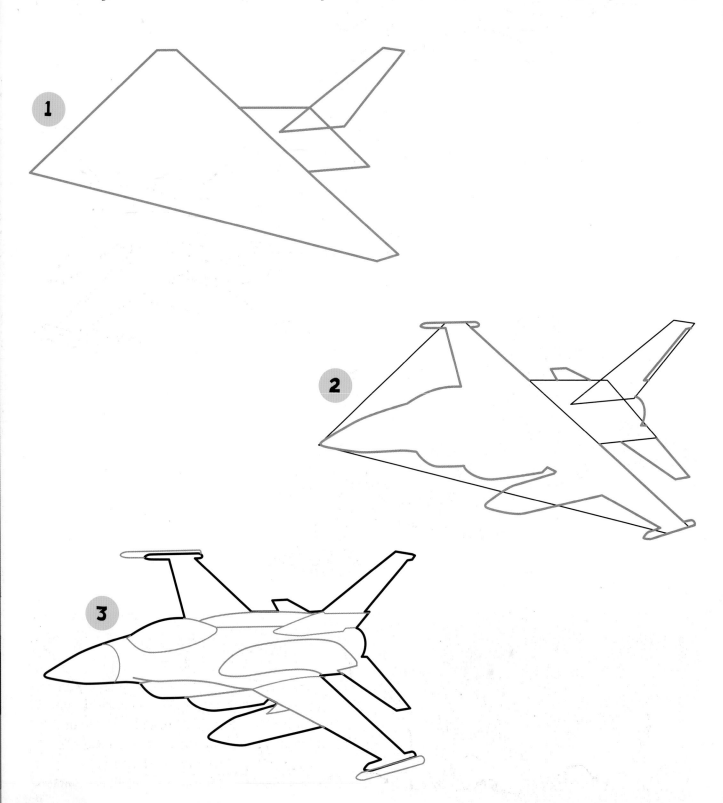

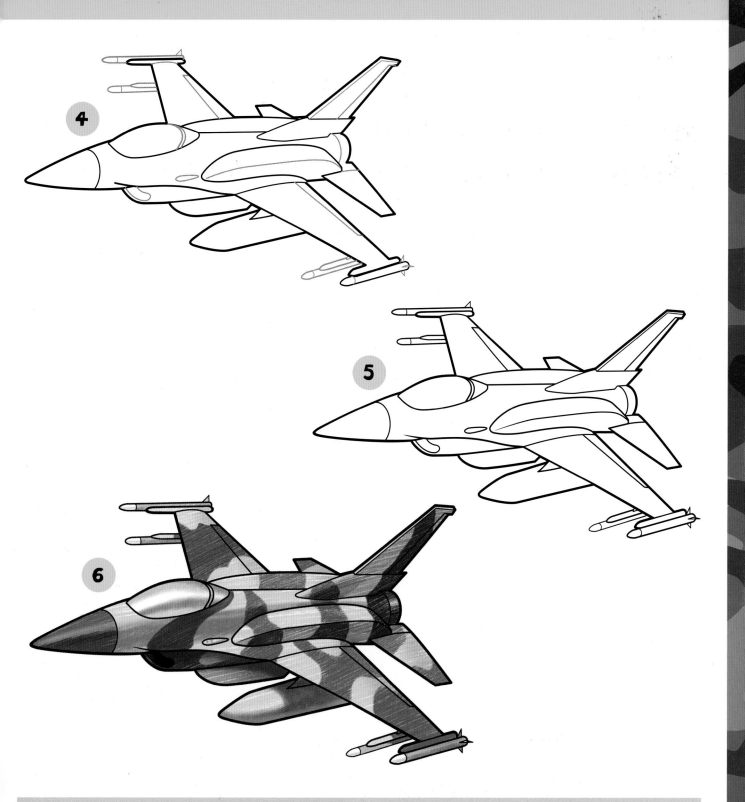

4

5

6

Fun Fact

The F-16 is loaded with an M61 Gatling-style gun. This piece of deadly artillery features a six-barrel 20mm cannon that fires 6,000 rounds per minute. The gun rapidly spins in a circle, which allows it to fire continuously without reloading.

Maritime Patrol Aircraft

This multipurpose plane is often used for search and rescue missions, as well as a variety of other functions.

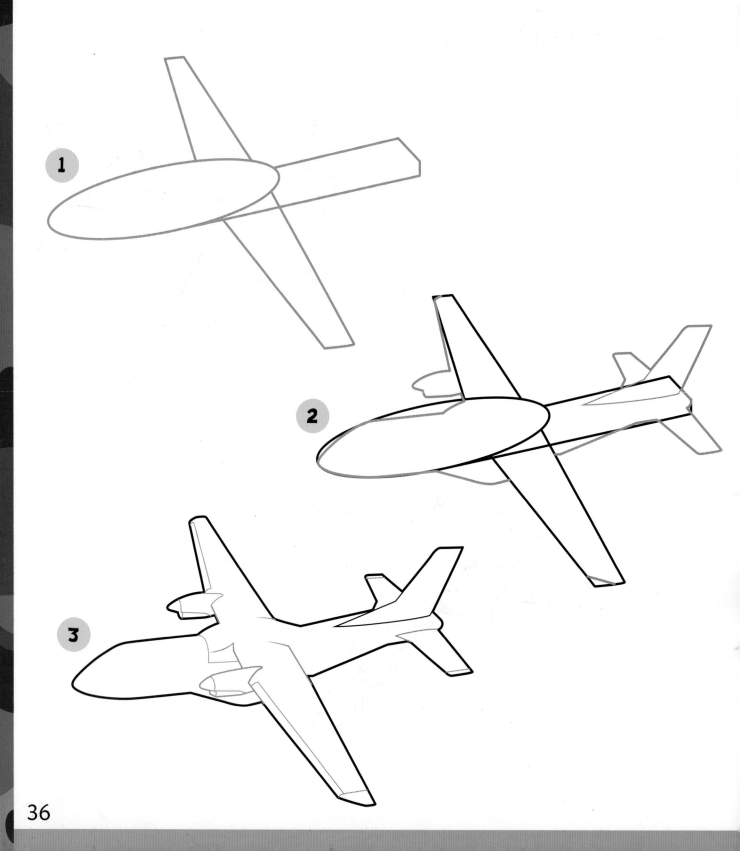

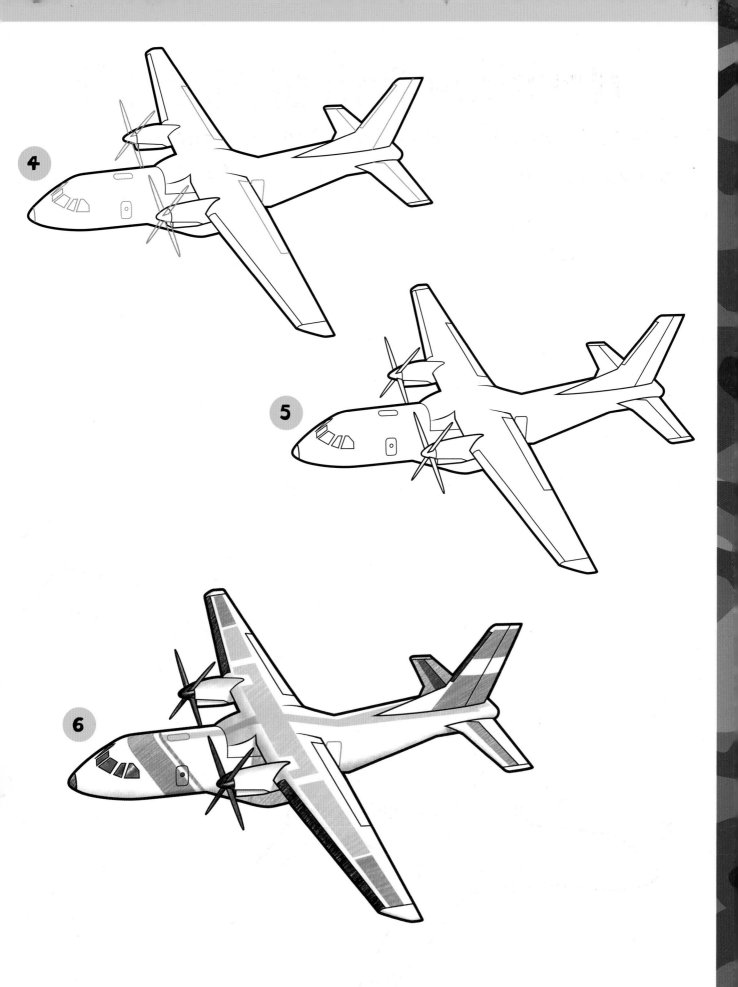

Nuclear-Powered Supercarrier

This enormous ship is used as a portable flight deck for up to 85 airplanes. Its flat deck is also a giant runway.

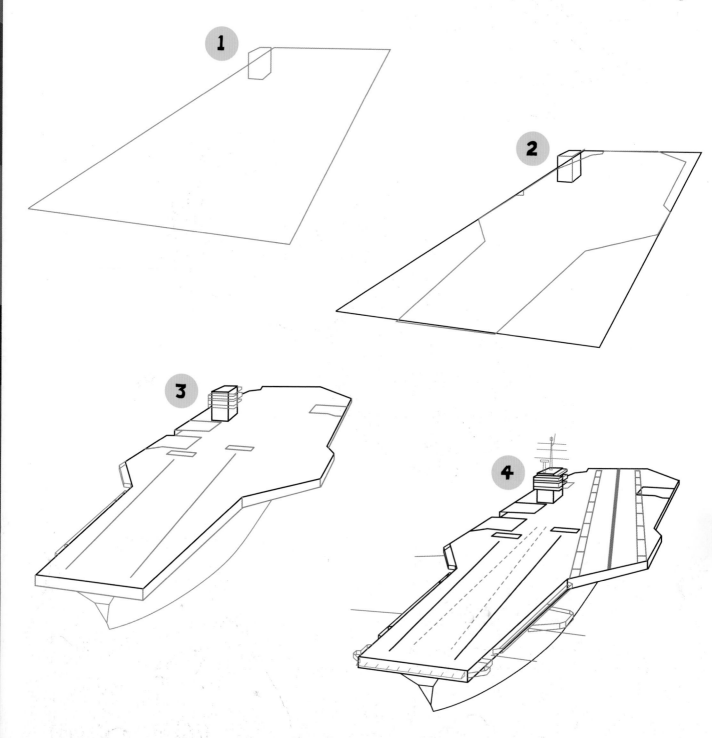

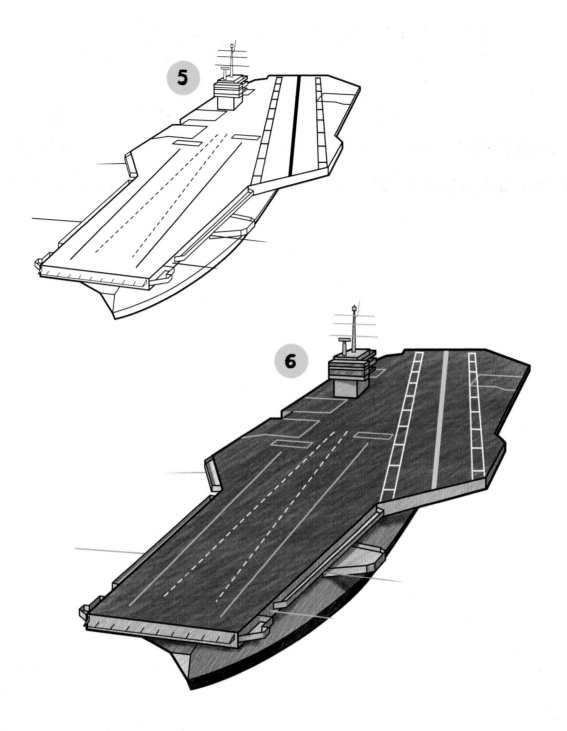

5

6

Fun Fact

This supercarrier runs on nuclear power. With its two nuclear reactors, it never has to stop for gas—it can run for 20 years without refueling!

Heavy Expanded Mobility Tactical Truck (HEMTT)

Nicknamed the "dragon wagon," this eight-wheel diesel truck can carry supplies, fuel tanks, and large artillery.

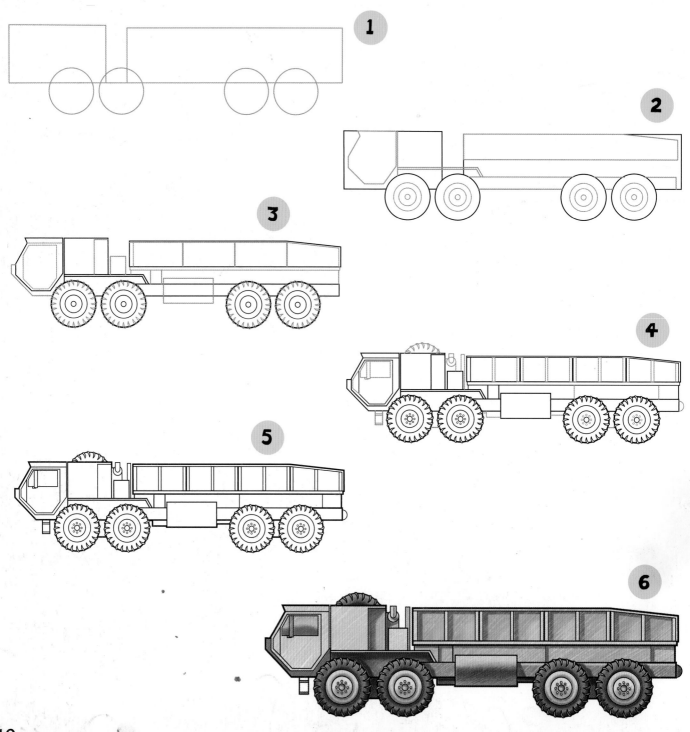

1

2

3

4

5

6